Lee Kelly

A Book of Gardens

Lee Kelly

Introductions by

Randal Davis & Kassandra Kelly

Contents

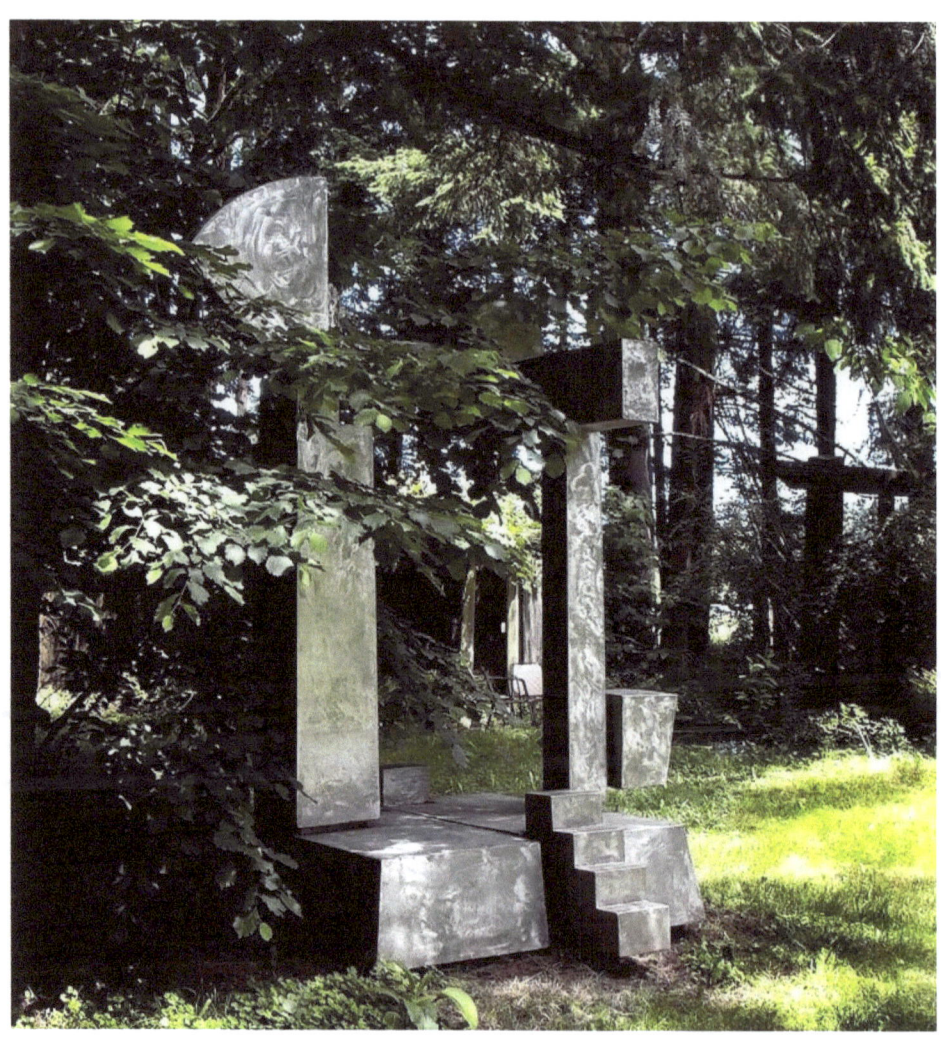

Patan (1996)

Stainless steel, 138 x 84 x 100 inches

Collection of the artist

I envision my work bridging the gap between individuals and the
environment. It creates a context, whether physical, political or spiritual, in which it is possible
for the viewer to re-examine his or her world. Perhaps for a few seconds, an individual may feel
that this place, this time, these people are part of a whole, and find a small piece of truth in our
shared world.

Lee Kelly 1997

A garden recreates nature and spirit in an image of the ideal.

Lee Kelly 1987

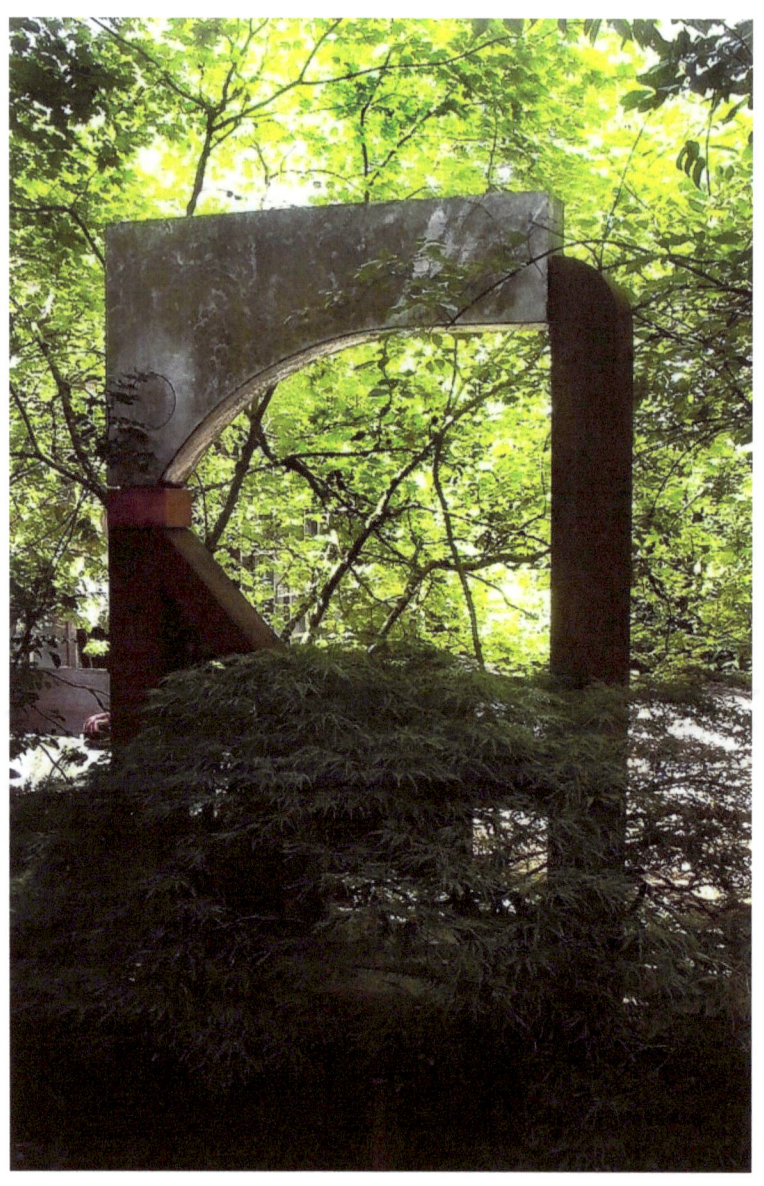

Red Gate (1982-1985)

Cor-ten steel, stainless steel, enameled steel

120 x 82 19 inches

Collection of the artist

Randal Davis   **"...looking in, looking out..."**

Lee Kelly's *A Book of Gardens*, self-published in 1987, occupies an interesting position in his body of work. As his career entered its third decade in the latter half of the 1970's and early 1980's, he had become widely known throughout the Northwest for highly visible public works in both Cor-ten and stainless steel. Such projects included monumental *Gate F* (1972) for San Francisco's Candlestick Park and *Leland I*, in collaboration with Bonnie Bronson, for Portland Center Park and the *Frank L Beach Memorial Fountain* in Portland's International Rose Test Garden (both 1975). This reputation was further secured by long-term outdoor exhibitions of major works at both Reed College (1976) and The Art Gym at Marylhurst University (1983).

By the early 1970's, Kelly's work had moved from the gestural vocabulary of Abstract Expressionism to a harder and reductive set of formal devices, a repertoire closer to the examples of David Smith and Anthony Caro. This transformation was largely complete by the end of the decade with works like *East of Riggins* (1978), *Nash* (1979) and *Manang* (1983), articulating qualities that would become salient features of his sculpture, explicitly architectural forms (albeit not necessarily "functional," in the strict sense) with an almost uncanny feeling of being at once artifacts of ancient past and a yet only glimpsed future.

With his first trek to Nepal in 1979, Kelly became, and remains, an inveterate traveler – India, Mexico, Viet Nam, Turkey, Burma – it might be more surprising if these journeys had no perceptible impact on his art, but that is hardly the case. Yet his work did not become some sort of transcultural pastiche, and that is what makes *A Book of Gardens* so interesting.

Surely most conspicuous is its breadth of reference. The first section of the book is a survey, in six pages, of the social function of the garden in Egypt, Persia, India, China and Japan. The remaining five pages are a summation and projection; notes and aphorisms mingle with suggestions of garden projects, some quite detailed, others better understood as proofs of concept. In fact, a very large number of these speculations came to inform finished works. The arch forms of "pavillion: a <gathering> place" [sic] found expression, at monumental scale, in the *Arch With Oaks* (1989), a commission for the Cornell Oaks Corporate Center, and at more intimate scale in *Akbar's Gate* (1988) and *Patan* (1996). The ground spirals (or "serpent waterways") have been a feature of many of Kelly's works, perhaps nowhere more explicitly than the *Interlocking Serpents* (1999) [left]. And when, on the final page of *A Book of Gardens*, Kelly writes of "symbols or devices to make connections... counterpoints to plant materials," we see the continuation of his fascination with the Yucatan ruins introduced to him in the early 1970's by architect, engineer and art dealer, John Bolles, and later brought to complete realization in, for example, *Icarus at Yucatan* (2005) [right].

So it's not hard to see that *A Book of Gardens* is important for its connections to Kelly's body of work. And you can glimpse that broader scope in his 1997 artist statement where "bridging the gap between individuals and the environment" requires "the viewer to re-examine his or her world." Put differently, it's been a commonplace of architectural history and theory since Vitruvius to speculate on the primal dwelling, the first principles of building. The most familiar form of this inquiry is Gottfried Semper's postulation of the four fundamentals of architecture: hearth, roof, wall and mound. He was, as Jonathan Hale has observed, "determined to go further back into the mists of pre-history if necessary, in his search for the ultimate forming principles in architecture."

In other words, it's archaeology and mythography at once. A thorough telling of Kelly's architectural tropes is another subject, one only hinted at here, but there is one sense in which the fact that the ruminations of

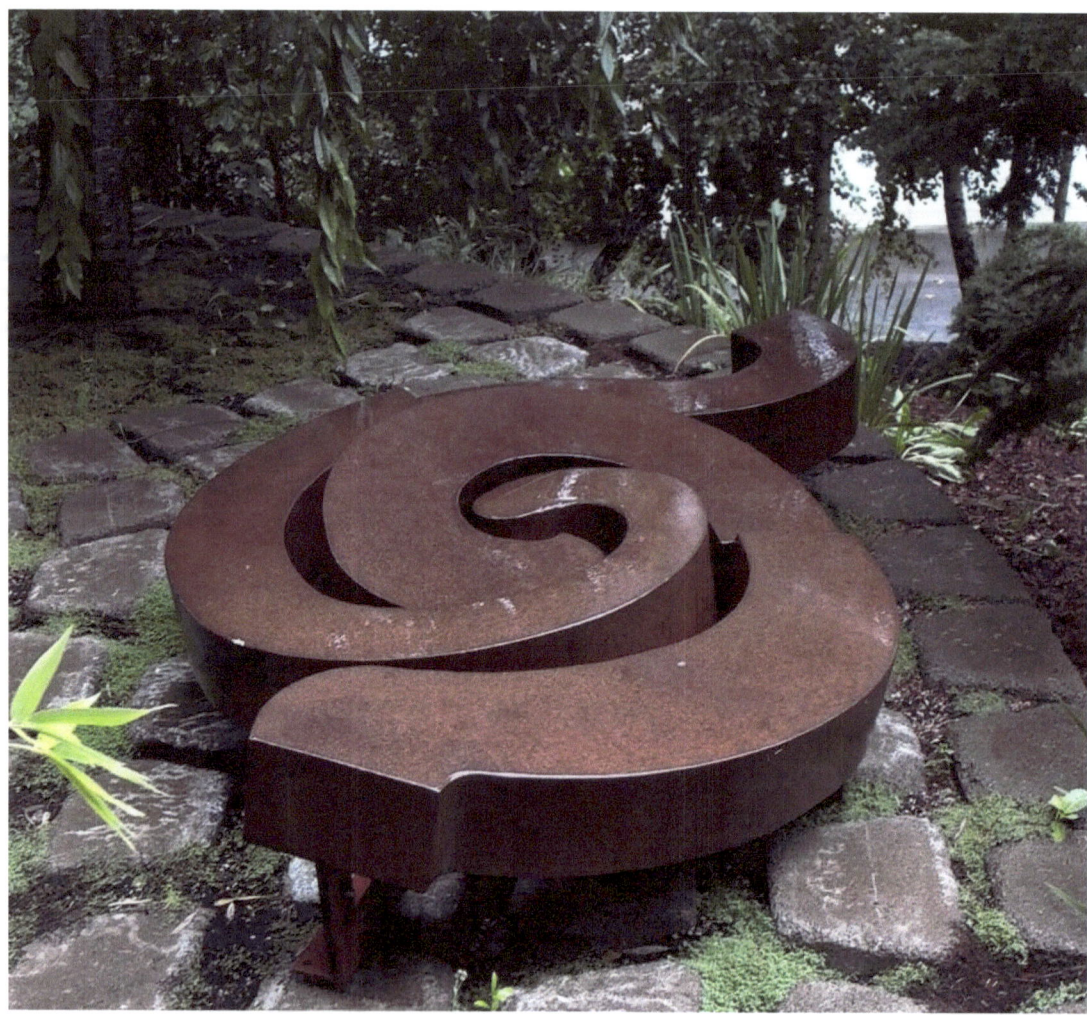

A Book of Gardens subsequently found substantial form may not be its most interesting aspect. *A Book of Gardens* is finally about first principles, less perhaps specifically architectural than purely phenomenological. Tom Turner has suggested that the first garden was a barrier placed in front of a cave, proof against "marauding beasts and brutes." The barriers pushed out, he suggests, protecting domestic animals and crops, finally becoming a site "to relax in the glorious sunshine of a Neolithic evening." You might read that as merely fuddled gentility, but there's something else there: the way in which one engages in the world, the necessity of boundaries between self and other, inner and outer, the expansion of that domain, and a final transformation to reflexivity.

What makes *A Book of Gardens* so interesting, then, is that its last words, "looking down into – looking out of" are not really the last. They were the first.

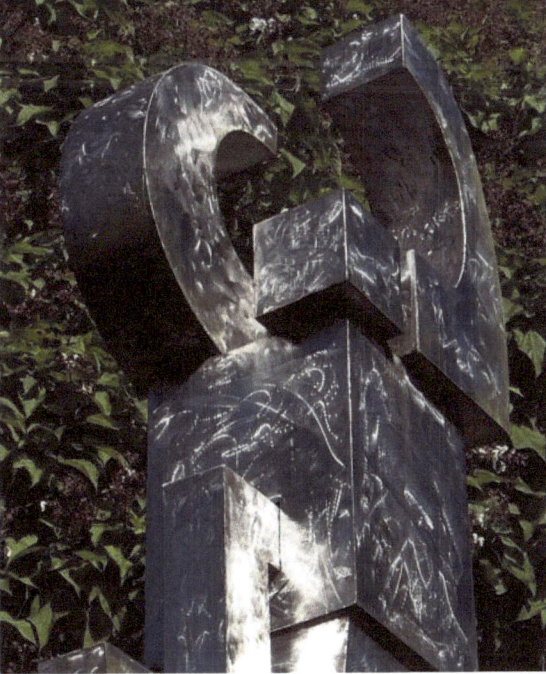

Opposite page:

Interlocking Serpents (1999)

Cor-ten steel.

Collection of Susan Hammer

Top and lower right:

Two views of *Icarus at Yucatan* (2005)

Stainless steel, 252 x 36 x 24 inches

Collection of the artist

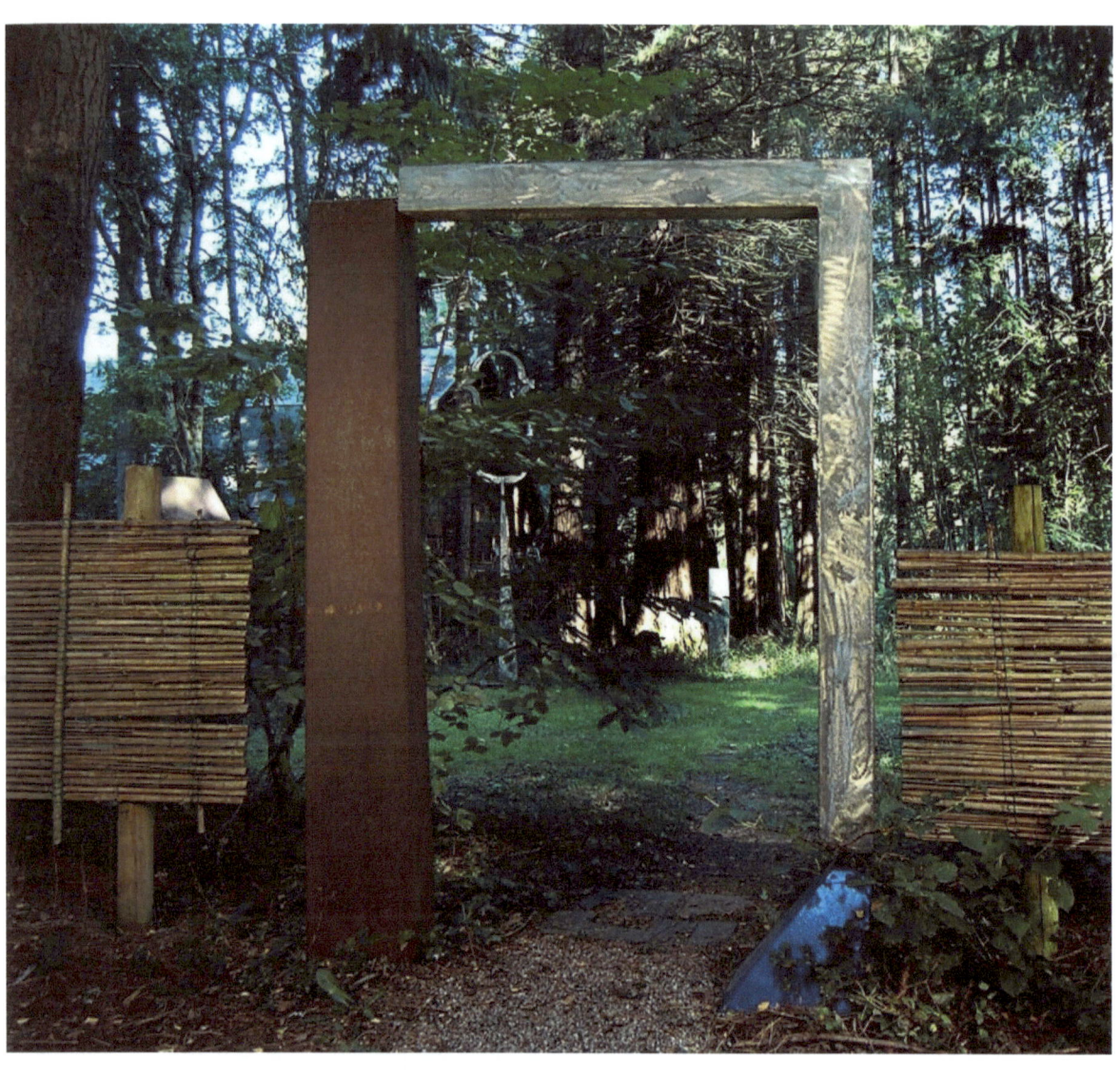

Borrowed Landscape (1987)

Cor-ten steel, stainless steel, enameled steel,

wood and bamboo, 101 x 250 x 30 inches

Collection of the artist

Kassandra Kelly   Borrowed Landscape

When Lee Kelly and Bonnie Bronson's garden book was made in 1987, they were exploring new sculptural environments. Making a living is always an up and down proposition for artists, but for Lee and Bonnie the down cycle often gave rise to innovation and new direction. In the mid 1980's they began composing gardens.

One of the ideas they explored is the principle of borrowed landscape, a tradition of Chinese design that incorporates background scenery into a garden composition. Lee's property, south of Oregon City, is a narrow slice of land bordered on the east and west by open pasture. Although you can stand on the east edge and see open pasture on the west, it is not easy to walk from one side to the other, even at the narrowest point. Bonnie and Lee expected that neighbors would build houses in the pastures, and so planted dense conifers along the fence lines, less to prevent others looking in but to keep us from looking out at our neighbors.

When Lee bought his first crane truck in 1972, parts of the property were suddenly available for siting large sculptures. Bonnie and Lee began to consider the relationships between sculptures as well as to the spaces within the garden. These were exterior living areas where daily rituals of drinking coffee and cocktails could occur outside while looking at sculpture and watching the seasons change.

It sounds simple–a bottle of wine in the garden with sculpture – but it engendered an attitude toward garden spaces that we continue to honor today. The property has islands of seating areas connected by walkways. The best seating areas provide a view further into the property, revealing spaces yet to be explored. Each site is better at certain times of day or year. Good for two people, four, or many. Some areas are intensely focused around the barn's work space – perfect for midday breaks. Others are high summer look-outs, hidden under a vaulted evergreen canopy; others take the full blast of sun. One place is for contemplation of winter where a reflecting pool brings light into the darkened landscape.

None are gardens for the sunset, which is to the west behind the hills rimming the valley. Late afternoons we watch sculptures catch the last light, holding the warmth of the day. Sculpture itself becomes a borrowed landscape, providing another view in exchange for what the garden must, by its very nature, wall out.

A Book of Gardens

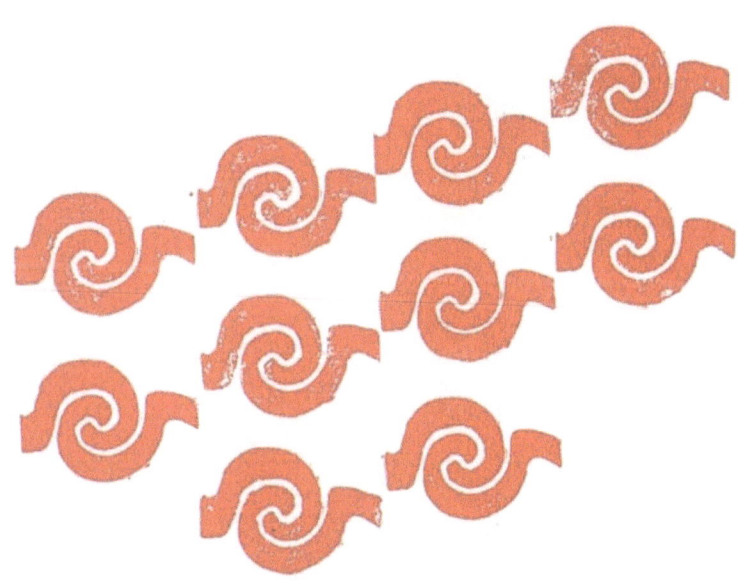

western tradition has it that man's first home
was a garden → east of eden ←
and we have tried to return ever since.

M Kelly · ©1987

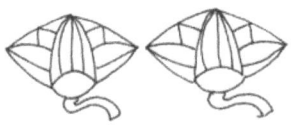 early garden: egypt

"prase to you nile
that comes from earth
to nourish egypt..
that waters the gardens..
she that re created to
nourish all cattle.."

 symmetrical plan, trees in rows
around water: oasis

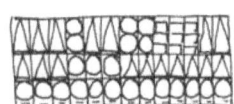

escape from summer heat - glare of cloudless
sky. garden as retreat - pool of water,
leafy trees.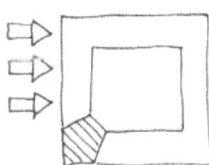

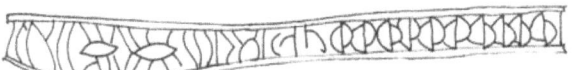

persia ⇨ paradise = garden, a concept universal to human experience, paradise as a garden.

reverence for water, mystical feeling for trees, ordering of nature

to transform desert
to represent the architecture of paradise

invention of garden objects: structures, columned halls, pavilions, water ways:
pools, basins
irrigation systems

waterchute - steps
↳to change levels between terraces.

india - pre mughal

rivers: ganga, yamuna holy waters bringing water from the himalaya, house of the gods.

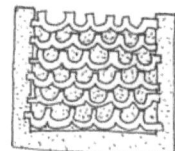

buddha attained perfect knowledge under a tree.

water- serpent kings (nagas), guardians of springs and holy tanks.
water- serpent device ∿ spiral ancient symbol.

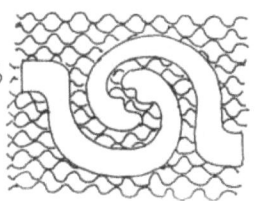

garden at night light/water flicker of light-sound of water

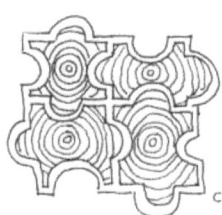

curbing @ anguri bagh

mughal-india

babur: soldier, garden-maker
"I laid out the four gardens (bagh-I-wafa)
on a rising ground, facing south,
there oranges, citrons, and pomegranates
grow in abundance"
"in order to bring water I had a large
channel dug."

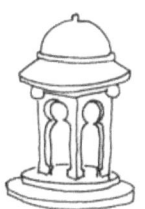

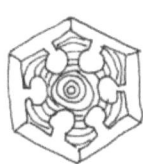

four gardens (charbagh) meeting,
baths, mosque.

"the best of young trees must be planted there,
lawns arranged, borders set with sweet-herbs."

water dominated, a place to be
alone or with family and friends.

pavilions to carry on life in a garden

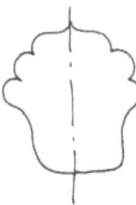

Japan

to capture a landscape : space, illusion

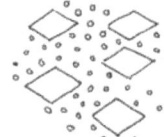 balance between nature and man

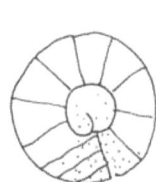

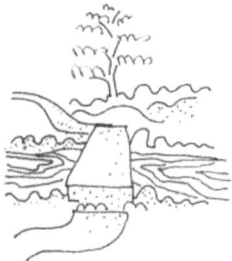

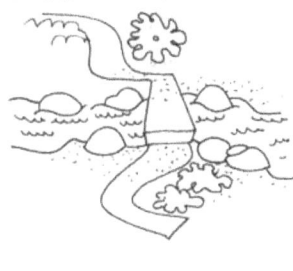

shakkei = borrowed scenery. landscape captured alive
example. framing a distant view to make it part
of the garden.

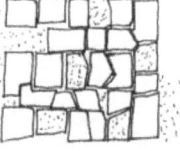

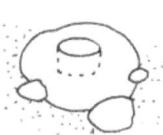

to choose a site w/ great natural beauty and
place something in it is not "borrowing scenery".

China
from vast nature preserves or hunting parks
to intimate family garden retreats from
the outside world, privacy behind a wall-
spaces recalling nature at its most wild and scenic

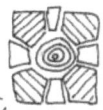

to make nature over◦ a piece of the wilds with architecture

covered passages
zig-zag path

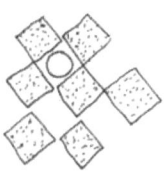

bridge
paving patterns
varied openings-doors-windows.
all weather experience of garden.

never going directly, always mystery of the unkown,
the garden slowly reveals itself.

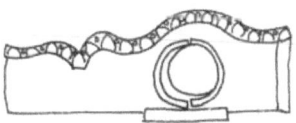

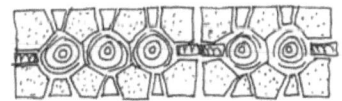

" a chinese garden is to be experienced,
one must physically move through the spaces,
only a hint of what lies around the corner
is revealed from any one point."

(david h engel- creating a chinese garden)

garden as a meeting place ⇨ between man and nature.

sculptural elements which
emphasize human presence.
leaves, water, bark, sky
all these things make
the surroundings.

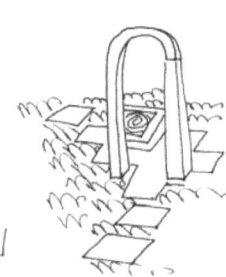

sculpture should
be human scale.
colors, textures
balance the natural
materials.

the working relationship between people
becomes critical to successfully making
sculpture for a garden

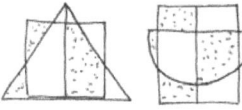

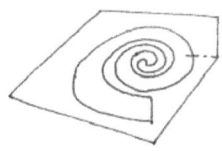

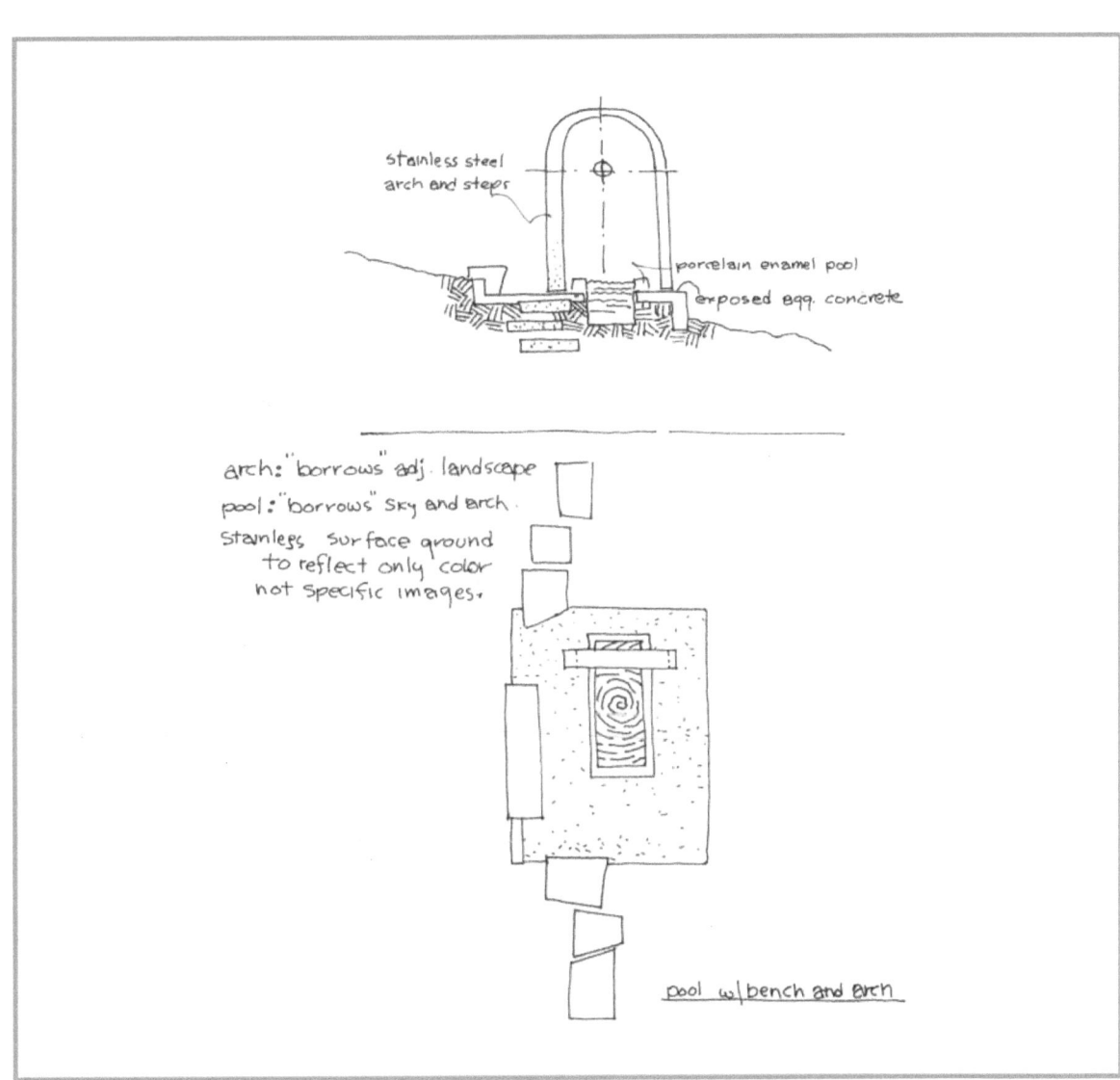

stainless steel
arch and steps

porcelain enamel pool

exposed agg. concrete

arch: "borrows" adj. landscape
pool: "borrows" sky and arch.
Stainless surface ground
    to reflect only color
    not specific images.

pool w/bench and arch

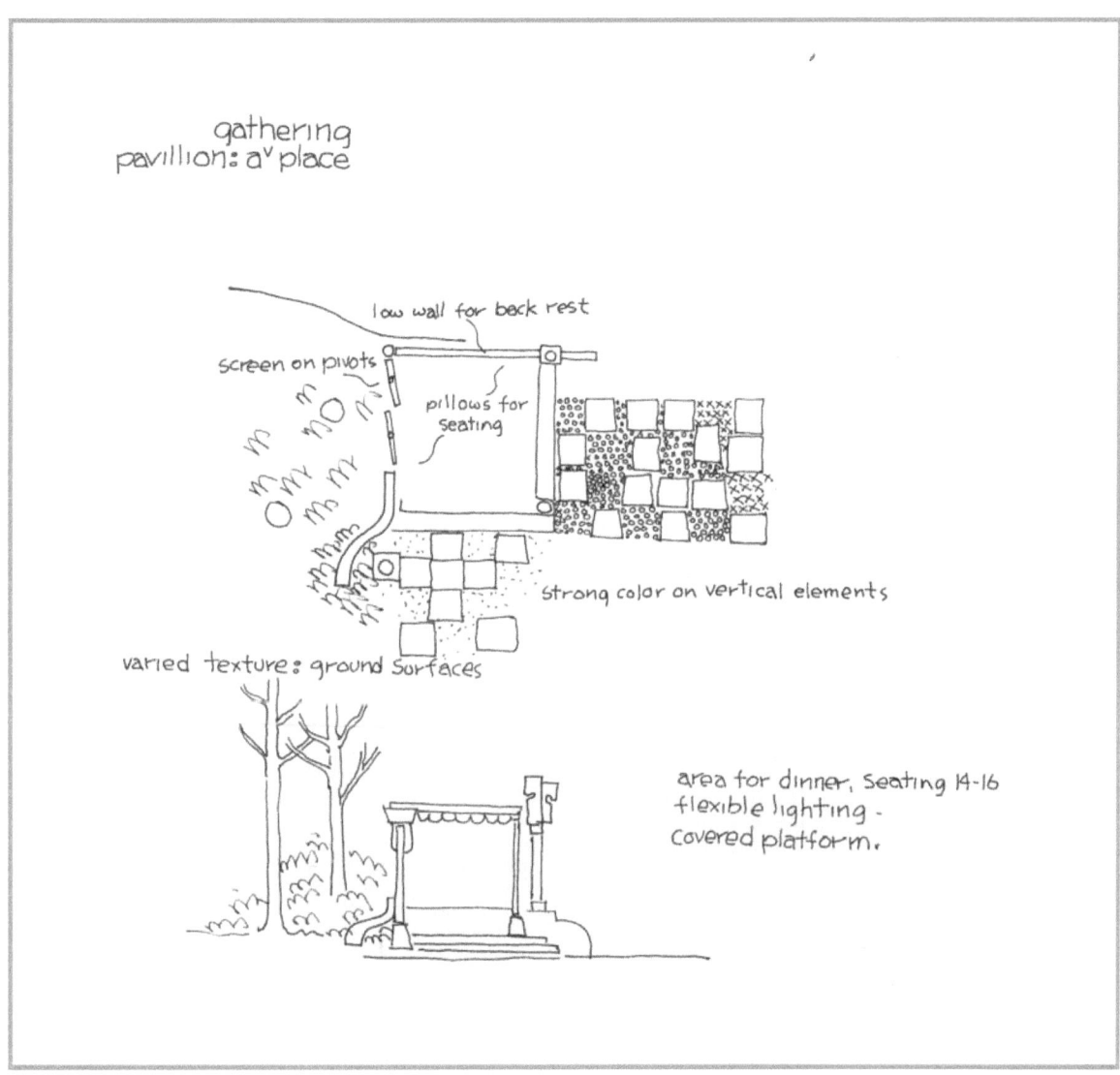

gathering
pavillion: a place

low wall for back rest

screen on pivots

pillows for seating

strong color on vertical elements

varied texture: ground surfaces

area for dinner, seating 14-16
flexible lighting -
covered platform.

serpent waterway

naga: benevolent snake-king
guardian spirit of water places

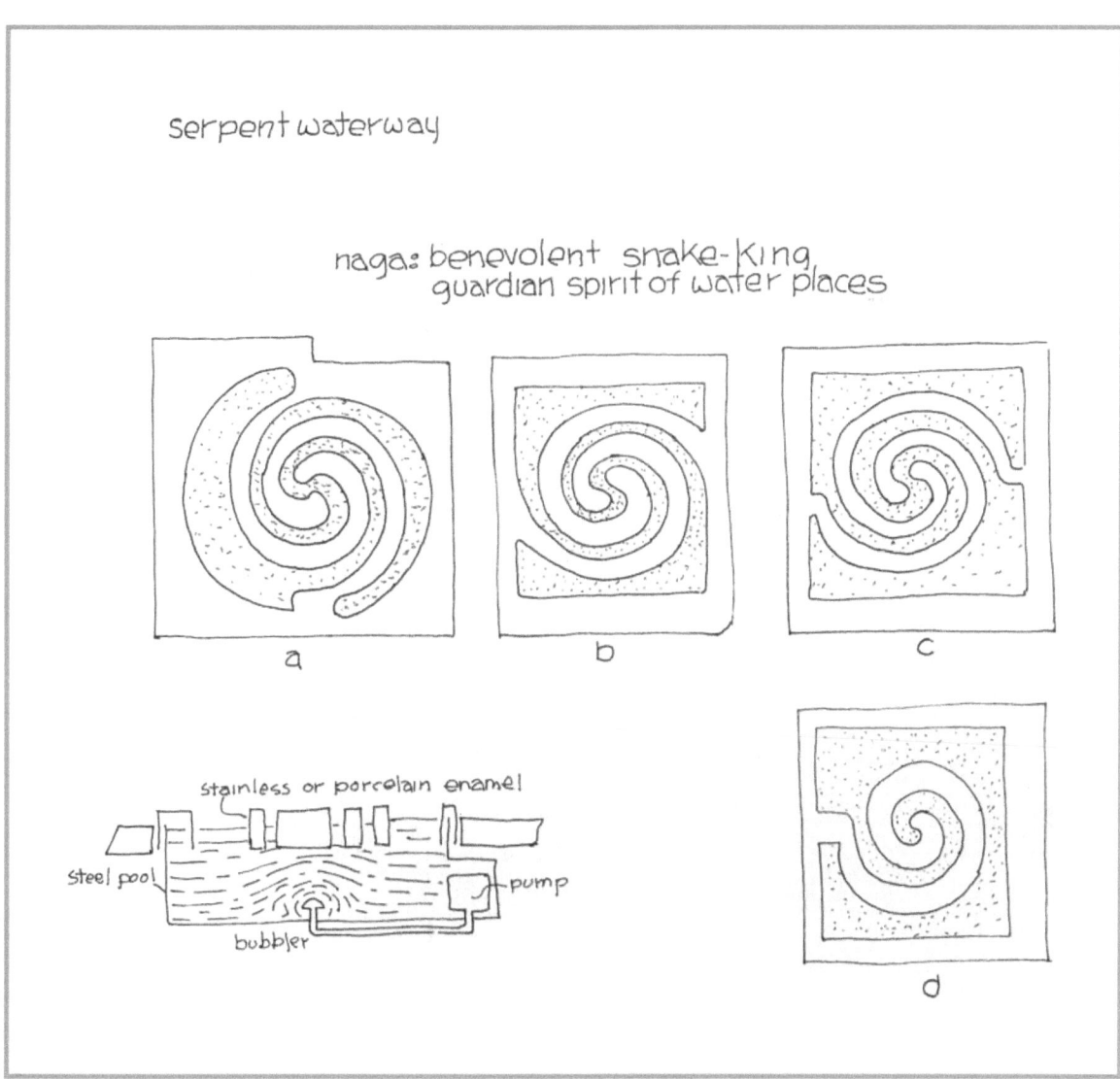

a

b

c

d

stainless or porcelain enamel

steel pool

pump

bubbler

a way to understand ourselves with nature
sculpture   symbols or devices to make connections.

as counter point to plant materials.

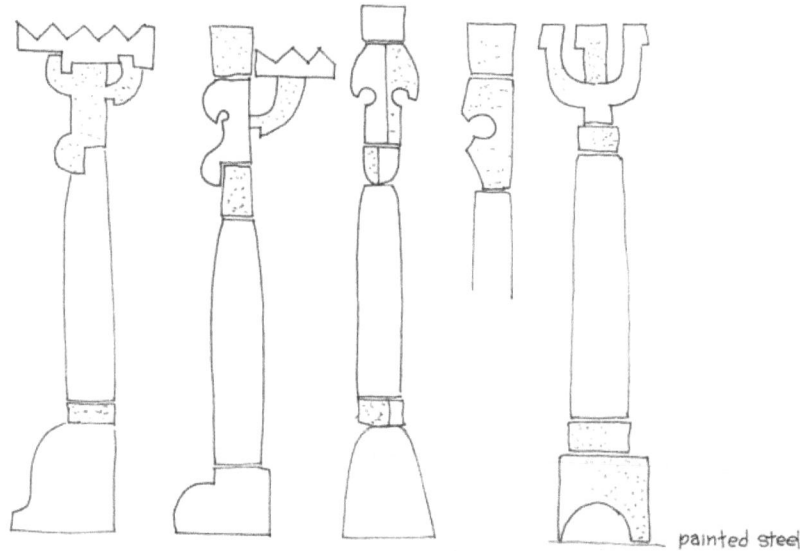

painted steel

garden at night and all seasons,
place for gathering, special events,
as well as daily life.
⇨ looking down into - looking out of.

Biography

Lee Kelly

Selected Solo Exhibitions, Commissions & Corporate Collections, 1990-2015

2012   Commission for *Celebes*, wall sculpture, Vestas Corporation, Portland, Oregon.

Purchase of *Memory 99,* Pacific Northwest College of Art & the Ford Family Foundation, Portland, Oregon.

Atacama, Elizabeth Leach Gallery, Portland, Oregon.

2011   Commission for *Moontrap*, wall sculpture, Rotary Club, Oregon City, Oregon.

Commission for *Rings*, Cor-ten steel sculpture, private residence, Portland, Oregon.

Maquettes, Elizabeth Leach Gallery, Portland, Oregon.

2010   *Lee Kelly: A Retrospective, Portland Art Museum*, Portland, Oregon.

Chrome Sculpture: 1967/2010, Elizabeth Leach Gallery, Portland, Oregon.

Purchase of *Sound Garden*, Art in Public Places, Bend, Oregon.

2009   *Reflections of Khajuraho*, Elizabeth Leach Gallery, Portland, Oregon.

Commission and purchase of *Bennington II* (2009) and *Blue Benn* (1998),

Washington State Arts Commission for Evergreen High School, Vancouver, Washington.

Commission for *Untitled*, Solheim residence, Portland, Oregon.

2008   *Doubtful Sound*, Elizabeth Leach Gallery, Portland, Oregon.

Commissioned stainless steel wall sculpture, West Portland Physical Therapy, Portland, Oregon.

Purchase of *Ship of Renewal I*, Saks Fifth Avenue, New York, New York.

2007   Elizabeth Leach Gallery, Portland, Oregon.

Civic Sculpture, B-Street Gallery, Portland, Oregon.

Commission for *Howard's Way*, The Civic, Portland, Oregon.

Commission for *Untitled*, Munch residence, Portland, Oregon.

Purchase of *Kyoto 3, 7, 9 & 10*, Bellevue Towers, Bellevue, Washington.

Purchase of *Kyoto 4*, The Casey Condominiums, Portland, Oregon.

Purchase of *Sulawesi VII*, Quimby Corporation, Portland, Oregon.

Commission for *Untitled*, Hockensmith & McCulloch residence, Portland, Oregon.

Commission for *Untitled* (Sulawesi Series), The John Ross Tower, Portland, Oregon.

2006   *Incidents of Travel: Sculptures and Works on Paper,* Elizabeth Leach Gallery, Portland, Oregon.

Commission for *Tahoe*, Lemelson residence, Incline Village, Nevada.

Commissioned stainless steel wall sculpture, Gustafson residence, Portland, Oregon.

Commissioned wall sculpture, Johnson residence, Portland, Oregon.

2005   *Icarus Revisited: New Sculpture*, Elizabeth Leach Gallery, Portland, Oregon.

Commission for *Loowit*, painted steel sculpture, Legacy Hospital, Vancouver, Washington.

Commission for *Fish Ladder*, sculptural fish ladder, Caldera, Blue Lake, Oregon, in collaboration with the Oregon Department of Fish and Wildlife.

Commission for *Sculpture in Two Parts*, Meridian Park Hospital, Tualatin, Oregon.

Commission for *Nelson Irrigation*, Walla Walla, Washington.

Commission for *Tri-Met #2*, Tri-Met, Beaverton, Oregon.

Outdoor installation of *Angkor Weep*, Quimby Welding, Portland, Oregon.

2004   Commissioned indoor fountain, Portland Community College, Sylvania Campus.

Commission for *Nancy's Garden*, private residence, Portland, Oregon.

Purchase of *Angkor IV*, Whitman College, Walla Walla, Washington.

Purchase of *Sulawesi VI*, M Financial, Portland, Oregon.

Commission of *Untitled in Three Parts*, Davis & Johantgen residence, Portland, Oregon.

2003   Purchase of *Canakkale*, stainless steel, Carol Woodruff Plaza, Richland, Washington.

Purchase of *Chalice I, II & III*, Gerding Edlen Development, Portland, Oregon.

2002   *Small Sculptures with Drawings*, Buckley Center Gallery, University of Portland, Portland, Oregon.

Commissioned stainless steel wall sculpture for exterior of Box and One Lofts, Portland, Oregon (Kevin Cavanaugh, Fletcher, Farr, Ayotte, architects).

Installation of two outdoor sculptures, *Lava Ridge* and *Four Columns*, Whitman College, Walla Walla, Washington.

2001   Commission for *Lupin Fugue*, stainless steel, Oregon Garden, Silverton, Oregon.

2000   *Travel Notes: Recent Sculpture*, Elizabeth Leach Gallery, Portland, Oregon.

Commission for *Powell Fountain*, Powell residence, Portland, Oregon.

Outdoor installation of *Lupin Study*, Hammer residence, Tacoma, Washington.

1999   *Trek to Sulawesi: Recent Wall Sculpture*, Fairbanks Gallery, Oregon State University, Corvallis, Oregon.

Commission for *Healing Place*, St. Vincent Hospital, Portland, Oregon.

Purchase of *Celebes Sea Snake Songs II*, FAIA, Portland, Oregon.

Purchase of *Celebes*, CTC Consulting, Portland, Oregon.

1998   *Recent Wall Sculptures*, Oregon State University, Corvallis, Oregon.

Ships of Renewal and Other New Work, Elizabeth Leach Gallery, Portland, Oregon.

Commission for *Bend Gate,* City of Bend, Oregon.

Commissioned sculpture, Sarkis residence, Seattle, Washington.

Purchase of *Naga*, Oregon State University, Corvallis, Oregon.

Purchase of *Sulawesi I*, Oregon State University, Corvallis, Oregon.

1997   Elizabeth Leach Gallery, Portland, Oregon.

1996   *New Print Editions*, 21 Steps Print Studio, Portland, Oregon.

Purchase of *Seljuk*, Cor-ten steel, Reed College, Portland, Oregon. Gift of Don Frisbee.

Purchase of *Angkor Series #1-94*, bronze over steel, Goodman residence, Portland, Oregon.

Purchase of *Untitled*, Stanford University Hospital, Palo Alto, California.

1995   Commission for *Stainless Dreaming*, Portland Community College, Rock Creek campus, Portland, Oregon.

Commission for *Salmon River,* for Portland-Sapporo Sister City Program. Sapporo, Japan.

1994   *Lee Kelly: 35 Years of Painting and Sculpture*, The Art Gym, Marylhurst College, Marylhurst, Oregon.

Purchase of *Summer Songs 1 & 2*, Fletcher, Farr & Ayotte, Portland, Oregon.

1993   *Collaborations in Steel and Sound*, Cheney Cowles Museum, Spokane, Washington.
With composer Michael Stirling.

Sound Garden, Elizabeth Leach Gallery, Portland, Oregon.

1992   *Tools of the Butter Trade*, Elizabeth Leach Gallery, Portland, Oregon.

Purchase of *Stainless Garden*, Stanford University, Palo Alto, California.

1991   Commissioned sculptural wall, Shipley residence, Portland, Oregon.

Commission for *Obelisk*, Wilson residence, Portland, Oregon. With composer Michael Stirling.

Commissioned sculpture, Schnitzer residence, Portland, Oregon. With composer Michael Stirling.

Purchase of *Summer Songs 5*, Ushio Oregon, Inc., Newberg, Oregon.

1990   Commission for *Friendship Columns*, North Waterfront Park, Portland, Oregon.
With composer Michael Stirling.

Lee Kelly
Selected Biography

2010   *Lee Kelly: A Retrospective*, Portland Art Museum, Portland, Oregon.

2008   Travel to New Zealand.

2006   Travel to Japan: Kyoto, Naoshima, Tokyo.

2006   Travel to Haida sites, Queen Charlotte Islands.

2005   Travel to Patagonia, Argentina & Chile.

2004   Travel to India & Sri Lanka.

2003   Travel to Anasazi sites, American Southwest.

2000   Travel to Burma and Nepal.

1994   Travels in Cambodia and Thailand. Visiting artist to Sapporo, Japan, as part of Portland-Sapporo Sister City Program.

        Lee Kelly: Retrospective of Painting and Sculpture, The Art Gym, Marylhurst College, Marylhurst, Oregon.

1992   Masters Fellowship in Sculpture, State of Oregon.

1987   Oregon Governor's Award for the Arts.

1985   Oregon Arts Commission Fellowship to research traditional bronze casting methods of the Newari people of Nepal.

1984   *Lee Kelly: Outdoor Sculpture*, The Art Gym, Marylhurst College, Marylhurst, Oregon.

1979   First visit to Nepal and India.

1976-79 Visiting Professor of Art, Reed College, Portland, Oregon.

Lee Kelly is represented by the Elizabeth Leach Gallery. For more information, visit www.elizabethleach.com.

www.ingramcontent.com/pod-product-compliance
Lightning Source LLC
Chambersburg PA
CBHW040750200526
45159CB00025B/1835